ABOUT THIS GUIDE

Backyard Birds of Western North America is based on the #1 birding website, AllAboutBirds.org, from the Cornell Lab of Ornithology. This guide is a pocket-sized companion to the newly released book, *All About Backyard Birds*, from the Cornell Lab Publishing Group.

Featuring 60 of the most commonly seen backyard birds of western North America, the illustrations and text in this guide highlight distinguishing features of each species.

You can also learn more by downloading the Lab's free Merlin® Bird ID app and by visiting AllAboutBirds.org to explore more information, images, and resources.

This title is one in a series of folding pocket guides that introduce you to basic birding skills, species identification, enhancement of backyard birding habitats, and more.

A NOTE ABOUT CITIZEN SCIENCE AND THE LAB

If you enjoy watching birds, we need your help. More than 400,000 people contribute to the Cornell Lab's citizen-science projects each year. Scientists use the data they collect to determine how birds are affected by habitat loss, pollution, and disease. They trace bird migration and document long-term changes in bird numbers continent-wide. The results have been used to create management guidelines for birds, investigate the effects of acid rain and climate change, and advocate for the protection of declining species. We invite you to be a part of our community and get started with a citizen-science project today. Visit birds.cornell.edu/citsci for more information.

DISCOVER A NEW WINDOW TO THE BEAUTY OF BIRDS WITH PROJECT FEEDERWATCH

Project FeederWatch is a winter-long survey of birds that visit feeders. We invite you to join by identifying and counting the birds at your feeders from November through April, learning about your feeder friends all the while. Using an easy online system, enter your counts and create colorful easy-to-understand graphs and summaries of the birds in your backyard.

Anyone interested in birds can participate. All you need is a window and a yard with feeders, plantings, and water to attract birds. Increase your enjoyment and knowledge of birds while contributing to science. Learn more and sign up at FeederWatch.org

The Cornell Lab of Ornithology

The Cornell Lab of Ornithology is a world leader in the study, appreciation, and conservation of birds. Our hallmarks are scientific excellence and technological innovation to advance the understanding of nature and to engage people of all ages in learning about birds and protecting the planet.

PLEASE VISIT US AT BIRDS.CORNELL.EDU

Published by Waterford Press
Text by the Cornell Lab of Ornithology, © Cornell University 2017
Editor: Kathi Borgmann. Bird illustrations © Pedro Fernandes
Colors and markings may be duller or absent during different seasons.
The measurements denote the length of birds from bill to tail tip.
Steller's Jay cover image © Shutterstock
Photographs are © as credited; uncredited photos
© Shutterstock. All rights reserved

Waterford Press produces reference guides that introduce novices to nature, science, travel and languages. Product information is featured on the website: www.waterfordpress.com

To order or for information on custom-published products, call 800-434-2555 or email info@waterfordpress.com

Made in the USA

ISBN 978-1-62005-243-3
$9.95 U.S.
9 781620 052433 50995
UPC 8 84682 01199 4
10 9 8 7 6 5 4 3 2 1 707803

BACKYARD BIRDS of WESTERN NORTH AMERICA

CORNELL LAB OF ORNITHOLOGY

The Cornell Lab of Ornithology

BACKYARD BIRDS *of* WESTERN NORTH AMERICA

A FOLDING POCKET GUIDE TO COMMON BACKYARD BIRDS

From the #1 Birding Website

ALLABOUTBIRDS.ORG

JAYS, CROWS, AND BLACKBIRDS

WOODHOUSE'S SCRUB-JAY
Aphelocoma woodhouseii
To 11.8 in (30 cm)

A lanky looking jay, light blue and gray above, with a whitish throat and grayish belly separated by an indistinct, partial breast band of blue.

STELLER'S JAY
Cyanocitta stelleri
To 13.4 in (34 cm)

Blue overall with a charcoal black head. Note prominent triangular crest which often stands nearly straight up from the head.

AMERICAN CROW
Corvus brachyrhynchos
To 20.9 in (53 cm)

Entirely black with a heavy, straight bill and short rounded tail.

RED-WINGED BLACKBIRD
Agelaius phoeniceus
To 9.1 in (23 cm)

A stocky blackbird with a conical bill and humpbacked silhouette. Male is black with red-and-yellow shoulder badges. Female is streaked brown with a whitish eyebrow.

BROWN-HEADED COWBIRD
Molothrus ater
To 8.7 in (22 cm)

Male has glossy black plumage and a rich brown head. Female is plain grayish-brown with fine streaking on the belly. Note thick finchlike bill.

BULLOCK'S ORIOLE
Icterus bullockii
To 7.5 in (19 cm)

Adult male is bright orange with a black back and throat, large white wing patches, and orange face with a black line through it. Female and young have a yellowish-orange head and tail, grayish back, and white wingbars.

JAYS, CROWS, AND BLACKBIRDS

BREWER'S BLACKBIRD
Euphagus cyanocephalus
To 9.8 in (25 cm)

Male is glossy black with a blue sheen on the head and a green sheen on body with yellow eyes. Female is brown with darker wings and tail and a dark eye.

GREAT-TAILED GRACKLE
Quiscalus mexicanus
To 18.1 in (46 cm)

Male is iridescent black with yellow eyes. Note long tail held in a V. Female is dark brown above, paler below.

CARDINALS, WAXWINGS, AND GROSBEAKS

NORTHERN CARDINAL
Cardinalis cardinalis
To 9.1 in (23 cm)

Male is brilliant red overall, with a thick reddish bill surrounded by black and a red crest. Female is pale brown overall with warm reddish tinges in the wings, tail, and crest.

CEDAR WAXWING
Bombycilla cedrorum
To 6.7 in (17 cm)

A sleek bird with a crest, a black mask, and an affinity for berries. Note yellow-tipped tail.

BLACK-HEADED GROSBEAK
Pheucticus melanocephalus
To 7.5 in (19 cm)

Stocky bird with large conical bill. Adult male is orange-cinnamon with a black head and black-and-white wings. Female and young are brown above with warm orange or buff on the breast.

EVENING GROSBEAK
Coccothraustes vespertinus
To 7.1 in (18 cm)

A heavyset finch with a large, conical, olive-colored bill. Note yellow eyebrow and white wing patches on male. Female is gray overall with white wing patch on dark wings.

THRUSHES AND ALLIES

AMERICAN ROBIN
Turdus migratorius
To 11 in (28 cm)

Gray-brown above with a warm orange belly and breast. Note yellow bill, faint streaking on throat, and white eye crescents. Female is similar but paler.

VARIED THRUSH
Ixoreus naevius
To 10.2 in (26 cm)

Male is dark blue-gray on the back and rich burnt-orange below with a sooty breastband and an orange line over the eye. Female is similar but paler.

WESTERN BLUEBIRD
Sialia mexicana
To 7.5 in (19 cm)

Male is shiny blue above with a rusty-orange color on the breast, flanks, and upper back. Female is gray-buff with a pale orange wash on the breast and blue tints in the wings and tail.

HERMIT THRUSH
Catharus guttatus
To 7.1 in (18 cm)

A small brown thrush with a reddish tail and pale underparts with distinctive spots on the throat and smudged spots on the breast.

NORTHERN MOCKINGBIRD
Mimus polyglottos
To 10.2 in (26 cm)

Overall gray-brown, paler on the breast and belly, with two white wingbars. Note white patch in the wings in flight. Conspicuous and vocal, mimics other songbirds.

STARLINGS

EUROPEAN STARLING
Sturnus vulgaris
To 9.1 in (23 cm)

Introduced to North America from Europe. Chunky, blackbird-sized with a short tail, iridescent purplish-green plumage, and yellow bill.

FINCHES

AMERICAN GOLDFINCH
Spinus tristis
To 5.1 in (13 cm)

Breeding male is bright yellow with a black forehead and black wings with white markings. Female is dull yellow beneath and olive above. Winter birds are unstreaked and brownish with dark wings and pale wingbars.

LESSER GOLDFINCH
Spinus psaltria
To 4.5 in (11 cm)

Male is bright yellow below with a glossy black cap and white patches in the wings; back can be black or dull green. Female and young have olive back, dull yellow underparts, and gray-black wings.

PINE SISKIN
Spinus pinus
To 5.5 in (14 cm)

A finely streaked finch with a sharp pointed bill and subtle yellow edgings on wings and tail.

HOUSE FINCH
Haemorhous mexicanus
To 5.5 in (14 cm)

Adult male is rosy red around the face and breast, with a streaky brown back, belly, and tail. Note red rump on male in flight. Adult female is plain grayish brown with thick, blurry streaks.

PURPLE FINCH
Haemorhous purpureus
To 6.3 in (16 cm)

Male has a pink-red head and breast and a streaky brown back. Female is heavily streaked and has a white eyebrow stripe.

CASSIN'S FINCH
Haemorhous cassinii
To 6.3 in (16 cm)

Male is rosy pink overall with brighter red crown. Female and juvenile are brown and white with crisp, dark streaks on the chest and underparts. Note streaks under the tail.

Oregon form

DARK-EYED JUNCO
Junco hyemalis
To 6.3 in (16 cm)

Plumage varies regionally, but in general note dark gray or black head and throat, white belly, pink bill, and white outer tail feathers that flash in flight.

SPOTTED TOWHEE
Pipilo maculatus
To 8.3 in (21 cm)

A sparrowlike bird with a thick triangular bill. Males are black above and on the breast, with warm rufous sides, and a white belly. Note white spots on dark wings. Female is similar, but is brown instead of black.

Nonbreeding
Breeding

CHIPPING SPARROW
Spizella passerina
To 5.9 in (15 cm)

In summer, clean and crisp, with frosty underparts, pale face, and black line through the eye, topped off with a rusty crown. In winter, subdued, buff brown with a pinkish bill.

HOUSE SPARROW
Passer domesticus
To 6.7 in (17 cm)

Male has a gray head, whitish cheeks, black bib, and rufous neck. Female is buffy brown with dingy underparts. Found in urban settings. Introduced from Europe.

Slate-colored form
Sooty form

FOX SPARROW
Passerella iliaca
To 7.5 in (19 cm)

Plumage varies regionally, brown or gray above with brown splotches on the flanks and the center of chest.

SONG SPARROW
Melospiza melodia
To 6.7 in (17 cm)

A bulky, streaky brown sparrow with thick streaks on chest and flanks. Note central breast spot. The head is striped russet on gray with dark triangular stripes bordering the throat.

WHITE-CROWNED SPARROW
Zonotrichia leucophrys
To 6.3 in (16 cm)

Gray and brown overall with large, bold black-and-white stripes on the head. Young birds have brown, not black, markings on the head.

AMERICAN TREE SPARROW
Spizelloides arborea
To 5.5 in (14 cm)

The rusty cap, eyeline, and unstreaked breast with a central dark spot help separate this winter sparrow from others.

HOUSE WREN
Troglodytes aedon
To 5.1 in (13 cm)

A tiny brown wren with a bubbly song and barred wings and tail. Often holds tail up.

BEWICK'S WREN
Thryomanes bewickii
To 5.1 in (13 cm)

A boisterous brown wren with a long white stripe over the eye. The back and wings are plain brown and the tail is barred black.

Audubon's

YELLOW-RUMPED WARBLER
Setophaga coronata
To 5.5 in (14 cm)

In summer, males and females are gray and black with white flashes in the wings and tail, and yellow on the crown, sides, and rump. In winter, birds are pale brown with a yellow rump and paler yellow sides.

RUBY-CROWNED KINGLET
Regulus calendula
To 4.3 in (11 cm)

A tiny songbird, olive-green above with a prominent white eyering and white wingbar that contrasts with adjacent blackish bar on the wing. Only males have the ruby crown.

RED-BREASTED NUTHATCH
Sitta canadensis
To 4.3 in (11 cm)

Small and compact, it creeps up and down trees. It has a slightly upturned bill and short tail. Blue-gray above, cinnamon below with a black cap, and black stripe through its white face.

WHITE-BREASTED NUTHATCH
Sitta carolinensis
To 5.5 in (14 cm)

Compact bird with very short tail. Creeps up and down trees. Gray-blue above and white below with a black cap and a white face. Note chestnut color under the tail.

BLACK-CAPPED CHICKADEE
Poecile atricapillus
To 5.9 in (15 cm)

A tiny, roundish songbird with a black cap and bib separated by stark white cheeks.

MOUNTAIN CHICKADEE
Poecile gambeli
To 5.5 in (14 cm)

Similar to Black-capped Chickadee but with a white stripe over the eye.

OAK TITMOUSE
Baeolophus inornatus
To 5.8 in (15 cm)

A plain gray-brown songbird with a short, stubby bill and short crest. They are slightly darker gray above than below.

BUSHTIT
Psaltriparus minimus
To 3.1 in (8 cm)

A tiny, kinglet-sized bird that is brown and gray above and paler below with a long tail and a short bill.

EURASIAN COLLARED-DOVE
Streptopelia decaocto
To 11.8 in (30 cm)

A light brown to gray-buff dove with a black crescent on the back of the neck. Tail tip is square, unlike Mourning Dove's pointed tail. Introduced from Europe.

MOURNING DOVE
Zenaida macroura
To 13.4 in (34 cm)

A plump dove with a long, pointy tail bordered in white. Tan overall with black spots on the wing.

WESTERN KINGBIRD
Tyrannus verticalis
To 9.4 in (24 cm)

A large flycatcher with a heavy bill, gray head, yellow belly, and whitish chest and throat. Note black tail with white outer tail feathers, conspicuous in flight.

SAY'S PHOEBE
Sayornis saya
To 6.7 in (17 cm)

A slender flycatcher that is pale brownish gray above with a cinnamon belly, a darker tail, and a gray breast.

TREE SWALLOW
Tachycineta bicolor
To 5.9 in (15 cm)

Streamlined swallow with pointed wings and short slightly notched tail. Male is blue-green above and white below. Female is brownish above and white below.

BARN SWALLOW
Hirundo rustica
To 7.5 in (19 cm)

An aerial acrobat that is dark blue above with rufous to tawny underparts and a cinnamon forehead and throat. Note long, forked tail in flight on adults.

SHARP-SHINNED HAWK
Accipiter striatus
To 13.4 in (34 cm)

Small, long-tailed hawk, slaty blue-gray above with narrow orange bars on the breast. The tail is barred and square-tipped.

COOPER'S HAWK
Accipiter cooperii
To 18 in (46 cm)

Medium-sized, long-tailed hawk with a bull-headed appearance that is steely blue-gray above and barred orange below. The tail is barred and rounded at the tip.

RED-TAILED HAWK
Buteo jamaicensis
To 26 in (66 cm)

Large hawk with broad, rounded wings. Highly variable; most are brown above and pale below with a dark bar on the front edge of the wing, visible in flight. Adults have a red tail. Juveniles have a banded brown-and-white tail.

RED-SHOULDERED HAWK
Buteo lineatus
To 24 in (61 cm)

Medium-sized hawk with broad, rounded wings and reddish-orange breast. Wings are checkered dark and white with red-orange shoulder patch. In flight, wingtips have pale crescents.

AMERICAN KESTREL
Falco sparverius
To 12.2 in (31 cm)

About the size of a Mourning Dove, this small falcon is rusty brown above with black spots on the back and vertical black marks on the sides of the face. Males have gray wings.

CALIFORNIA QUAIL
Callipepla californica
To 10.6 in (27 cm)

Plump, small-headed game bird with a black face outlined with bold white stripes and single plume of feathers on the head. Note white, cream, and chestnut scales on belly.

HAIRY WOODPECKER
Picoides villosus
To 10.2 in (26 cm)

Larger with a longer bill than similar Downy Woodpecker. Bill is nearly same length as the head. Note white outer tail feathers. Only male has a red patch on the head.

RUFOUS HUMMINGBIRD
Selasphorus rufus
To 3.5 in (9 cm)

Male is bright orange on the back and belly with a vivid iridescent red throat. Female is green above with rufous-washed flanks, rufous patches on a green tail, and an orange spot on the throat.

DOWNY WOODPECKER
Picoides pubescens
To 6.7 in (17 cm)

Smaller with a shorter bill than the Hairy Woodpecker. Note black barring or spots on outer tail feathers. Only male has a red patch on the head.

ANNA'S HUMMINGBIRD
Calypte anna
To 3.9 in (10 cm)

Male and female have straight bills, green backs, and grayish-green bellies. Male has a reddish-pink head and throat. Female has a small central reddish-pink patch on the throat.

Red-shafted form

NORTHERN FLICKER
Colaptes auratus
To 12.2 in (31 cm)

A large brownish woodpecker with a black face outlined with bold white stripes and single plume of feathers on the head. The undersides of the wing and tail are yellow in the East and red in the West.

BLACK-CHINNED HUMMINGBIRD
Archilochus alexandri
To 3.5 in (9 cm)

Dull metallic green above and dull grayish-white below. Flanks are glossed with dull metallic green. Male has black throat with thin iridescent purple base. Female has pale throat. Bill is black.